BEADWORK.
Creates
Beaded Rings

BEADWORK®
Creates

Beaded Rings

Edited by
Jean Campbell

INTERWEAVE PRESS

Printed and bound in China by Asia Pacific

Editor: Jean Campbell
Copy editor: Christine Townsend
Technical editor: Laurie Shimuzu Freeman, Jean Campbell
Book design: Paulette Livers
Illustrations: Dustin Wedekind
Photo styling: Paulette Livers
Photography: Joe Coca
Book production: Samantha L. Thaler, Paulette Livers
Proofreader: Nancy Arndt

Library of Congress Cataloging-in-Publication Data

Campbell, Jean.
  Beadwork creates beaded rings : 30 designs / Jean Campbell.
    p. cm.
  ISBN 1-931499-26-8
  1. Beadwork. I. Title.
  TT860.C365 2004
  745.594'2--dc22
                                        2004003764

10 9 8 7 6 5 4 3 2 1

INTERWEAVE PRESS
201 East Fourth Street
Loveland, Colorado 80537-5655 USA
www.interweave.com

Dear Reader,

"Beaded what? Rings?" You may have said those words to yourself when you picked up this book. "Would they fall apart?" you wondered. "Do I have to spend a lot of time and money on a single piece of jewelry?" you pondered.

I'm here to set the record straight, because beaded rings are not only the hottest new fashion craze, they are also inexpensive and quick to make. And, by using some of the new fishing lines, elastics, and wire on the market, most are quite durable, even with hand-washing.

Beadwork Creates Beaded Rings is a compilation of thirty of the most exciting ring designs I've encountered. You'll find cocktail rings and everyday rings, sparkling crystal ones as well as sedate seed-beaded ones, rings you make to fit tightly on your finger and those that stretch easily over a knuckle. There are rings you knit, rings you work with a needle and thread, rings you bend with wire, and others you hold together with elastic. And you know what? All of them are gorgeous!

As with all of our Beadwork Creates books, it's a good idea to check our Techniques section on page 105 before you begin. It's full of great tips to start you on your way, and it contains all the stitch information you'll need for making each ring.

So sit down, find a favorite ring, and get to work. Before you know it, you'll need more than ten fingers to show off your new obsession.

—Jean Campbell
Editor-in-Chief
Beadwork magazine

nts

Lucky Scrunchie Ring

Jamie Hogsett

This ten-minute project will get you hooked on making rings!
It is flashy and stylish, but also easily glides over any finger
making it very comfortable.

Materials

- 44 sterling silver heishi spacer 4mm beads
- 2 Swarovski crystal 6mm rondelle beads
- 1 Swarovski crystal 8mm round bead
- 1 sterling silver 1mm crimp tube
- 6" of clear .05mm stretch elastic

Notions

Chain-nose pliers or crimping pliers

Step 1: Use the elastic to string 22 heishi spacers, 1 rondelle,
1 crystal, 1 rondelle, and the remaining spacers.

Step 2: String the crimp tube and pass through the first several
spacers you strung in Step 1. Gently pull both ends of the elastic to snug all the beads. Crimp the tube using the chain-nose
or crimping pliers. Trim both ends close to the crimp tube.

Jamie Hogsett is projects editor for Beadwork *magazine.*

Inner Light Ring

Jeannette Cook

Inspired by those wonderful Miyuki color-lined teardrop beads, this gorgeous ring is designed to wow your admirers. Show off your inner power with pride!

Materials

Orange color-lined drop beads
Red and olive Delica beads
½ of a cotton ball
1" × 1" piece of white grosgrain ribbon
Orange size B Nymo or A Silamide beading thread
Beeswax or Thread Heaven

Notions

Size 12 beading needles
Scissors
Pen
Lighter

Step 1: Draw a circle about the size of a quarter on the ribbon. Thread the needle with 3' of doubled and conditioned thread. Use running stitch to sew on the line you just made on the ribbon. Cut around the circle about ⅛" from the stitching. Use the lighter to carefully singe the fraying edges.

Step 2: Pull the ends of the thread to slightly draw in the sides of the circle. The ribbon will cup. Roll the cotton ball in your fingers to tighten it. Stuff it into the cup of ribbon and continue pulling the thread to tighten it around the cotton ball. Use your scissors end to tuck any loose cotton back into the ribbon as you tighten it. Gather the seam outside the stitching and tack them all down neatly. Rub this end on a flat surface to make it as flat as possible.

Step 3: Use your needle to pass up to the top center of the ribbon (the smooth end). String 1 drop and pass back through the fabric and out as close to where you exited as possible. Pull tight to seat the drop close to the fabric. Continue adding drops in concentric circles as tightly together as possible until you have covered all but the flattened end of the ribbon ball. Set aside.

Step 4: Using 3' of single conditioned thread, weave a piece of peyote stitch (see "Techniques," page 105) 14 beads wide and 8 beads tall. Work 4 more rows, decreasing on each side of the beadwork. Weave through the beads to the first row created in this step and make identical decreases. This piece will be the mount for your ring top.

Step 5: Making sure your thread is always hidden within the beads, continue working peyote stitch off of the mount. Do so by working with red beads 6-wide. This will create the band of your ring. Work the band until the entire ring fits comfortably around your finger.

Step 5: Connect the end of the band to the other side of the ring mount so they lock like a zipper and weave the beads together. Weave through all the beads on the band to reinforce, finishing near the center of the ring mount.

Step 6: Center the beaded ribbon ball on the mount and securely stitch it to the peyote stitch. Secure the thread and trim close to the work.

Jeannette Cook has been working with beads as a wearable and fine art form for thirty-five years and teaching beading workshops for eighteen years. She is owner of Beady Eyed Women® and can be reached at www.beadyeyedwomen.com.

Crystal Visions Ring Band

Susan J. Manchester

This sparkly crystal band is a great off-loom project for first-timers. Put it on and no one will know how easy it was to make!

Materials

    12 Swarovski crystal 4mm bicone beads
    Size 11° metallic-finish seed beads
    Monofilament fishing line, 4lb test

Notions

    Size 10 beading needle
    Scissors

Step 1: Using 1 yd of line, string 5 size 11°s. *String 1 crystal and 1 seed bead. Repeat from * five times. String 1 crystal.

Step 2: String enough size 11° seed beads so that all of the strung beads fit around your finger. (For ring sizes 5–6, you will string 20 size 11° seed beads to complete the band; for sizes 7–8, 23 seed beads; for sizes 9–10, 26 seed beads.) After testing for fit, increase or decrease by 3 seed beads as needed. Use a square knot to tie the beads into a circle leaving a 6" tail.

Note: It's important to keep the tension tight as the beads are worked into the ring band. When working the band in Row 2 (see chart), keep working on the same side of Row 1. Don't flip the work. Refer to Figure 1 for the stringing path.

Step 3: Pass back through the first 2 beads strung in Step 1.

Step 4: String 3 seed beads and 1 crystal. Pass through bead 6 (marked on Figure 1).

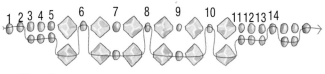

Figure 1

Step 5: String 1 crystal, 1 seed bead, 1 crystal. Pass through bead 10.

Step 6: String 1 crystal and 3 seed beads. Pass through bead 14.

Step 7: String 3 seed beads. Skip the next 3 seed beads in the band and pass through the next seed bead. Continue stringing 2 seed beads, skipping 2 beads, and passing through the third seed bead in the circle until the band is completed.

Step 8: Weave through all of the beads in the band to strengthen it. Tie a slipknot between crystals, pass though the crystal, and pull tight to hide the knot. Trim the thread close to the work. Finish by weaving the tail into the work and trimming it close to the work.

Susan Manchester is a corporate executive from Mound, Minnesota, who is eagerly awaiting retirement so she can spend more time beading and teaching bead classes.

White Bricks Ring

SuZ Garcia

If you know peyote stitch, this ring is quite easy to make. The pretty focal bead used on this ring is a vintage one, but you can use any type of flat-backed bead. When you change the focal bead you change the entire character of the ring, so choose your seed beads accordingly.

Materials

 6mm–8mm flat-backed focal bead (pearl, Czech fire-
  polished bead, crystal, lampworked bead, etc.)
 Size 8°, 10°, and 15° seed beads
 Size 11° triangle beads in a color to complement the
  seed beads
 Size 15° round seed beads or Delica beads
 Fireline 6lb test or other waterproof fishing line

Notions

 Size 12 sharps or beading needle
 Scissors

Step 1: Stretch 1 yd of line and thread it on the needle. String the focal bead and slide it to the middle of the line.

Step 2: String enough size 15°s to cover a third of the side of the focal bead. String an even number of triangles to cover a third of the side of the focal bead. String enough size 15°s to cover the remaining third of the side of the bead. Pass through the focal bead again (Figure 1). If you have a large-holed bead, your size 15°s may slide into the focal bead's hole. If so, fill the hole with the size 15°s and continue stringing.

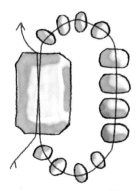

Figure 1

Step 3: Pass through the first size 15°s and the triangles you strung in Step 3. Work peyote stitch (see "Techniques," page 105) over the triangles only for 2 rows using triangle beads, 2 rows using the size 8°s, and 2 rows using the triangles.

Step 4: Weave through all the beads again until you pass through the focal bead. Pass through a few size 15°s surrounding the focal bead. Tie a knot between beads, pass through several more beads and trim the thread close to the work.

Step 5: Thread the needle on the other end of the thread and repeat Steps 2–4, but don't cut the thread.

Step 6: Work a strip of peyote stitch off of the triangles using size 15°s or Delicas or a mix of both. Make the strip long enough so that when you wrap the entire piece of beadwork around your finger it fits.

Step 7: Fit the ends of the ring band together so it creates a circle and the beads lock together like a zipper. Pass back and forth through the beads on each end to make a strong connection. Secure the thread and trim it close to the work.

Former costumer SuZ Garcia started seriously beading in 2000 to help her friend Denice Girardeau get a bead society started in Pittsburgh, Pennsylvania. Obsessive/Compulsive Beadworkers of PA (OCBPA) was born, and so was her continuing passion for beadwork. Now if she works on a costume, it's just to do the beadwork! Contact her at starfirebeads@aol.com.

Ab Fab Ring Band

Sharon Bateman

Here's a beautiful and simple ring made with tubular peyote stitch. Learn how to make the ring using this pattern, and then branch out to create your own!

Materials
  3 colors of Magnifica beads—A, B, and C
  Silamide thread

Notions
  Size 12 beading needle
  Ring mandrel
  Scissors

Note: When working a ring size that isn't a multiple of the 4-bead pattern, you'll end up creating one section without a complete pattern. Work the last rows of these sections on both sides of the ring in a solid color.

Step 1: Measure and cut 2 yd of thread. Measure 24" from one end of the thread and tape it to the ring mandrel at your ring size. String enough A beads to wrap around the mandrel. Pass through the first 2 beads strung to form a circle.

Step 2: Work three rounds of tubular peyote (see "Techniques," page 105) using A beads. Be sure to step-up in each round. If you wish, ease the ring off of the mandrel after completing the third round. Leave the tape on the thread.

Step 3: Work a round of tubular peyote, alternating one-drop A with two-drop B (you will be making an increase).

Step 4: Work a round of one-drop tubular peyote using B all around.

Step 5: Work a round of tubular peyote, alternating two-drop C and one-drop B.

Step 6: Secure the thread and trim close to work. If you have not already done so, remove the ring from the mandrel, and take the tape off of the tail. You will use this tail to complete the other side of the ring.

Step 7: Work a row of tubular peyote, alternating one-drop A and two-drop B all around. Make sure the two-bead sets of this round line up with the two-bead sets on the edge of the opposite side.

Step 8: Work a round of one-drop tubular peyote using B.

Step 9: Sew the edges of the ring together by passing through the beads of the first side. Secure the thread and trim close to work.

Sharon Bateman lives in northern Idaho and has been beading professionally since the early 1990s. She can be reached for questions or comments at www.sharonbateman.com.

Simplicity Ring

Sandy Amazeen

If you have swollen knuckles and have sworn off ring-wearing, this knitted ring made with stretch cord is the answer to your prayers! And making one just might inspire you to use up that bead soup piling up on a corner of your beading table.

Materials

- Bead soup that includes size 6 and 8 seed beads, 4mm accent beads, minidrops, and minidaggers
- 16 matching small accent beads
- One spool of 0.5mm clear stretch cord
- Silamide thread to complement the beads

Notions

- 4" size 0 double-pointed knitting needles
- Zap-A-Gap or other quick-drying super glue
- Big Eye needle
- Beading needle

Note: These instructions assume a basic knowledge of bead knitting.

Step 1: String 20" of assorted beads from your bead soup onto the cord. Tie an overhand knot and fit it snugly onto one of the knitting needles. Add a drop of glue to the knot and allow it to dry. Cast on three stitches, sliding three beads in between each stitch.

Step 2: Knit a row, sliding three beads down to the working needle with each stitch. Some of the beads may slide out of place, but these won't show in the finished ring.

Continue to knit row by row until the desired ring diameter is reached. Cast off the three stitches and weave the ends of the ring together using a Big Eye needle and the cord. Draw these stitches together so that the ring narrows a bit at this grafting site. This slightly narrower section will create a comfortable fit at the underside of the finger. Add a drop of glue to the knot. Using the Big Eye needle, weave the tails and trim the ends.

Step 3: Use a beading needle to thread 24" of double-stranded Silamide. Find the top center of the ring. Count two raised rows from the center and secure the thread. *Pass through a seed bead, string 1 accent bead and 1 seed bead. Pass back through the accent bead. Pass through two adjacent beads on the base of the ring and repeat from * until you have embellished the ring with 3 beads per row for 5 rows. Secure the thread and trim it close to the work.

Sandy Amazeen is a frustrated painter who taught herself weaving, spinning, knitting, stained glass, and jewelry making while traveling the continent. What refuses to come out of her head to appear on canvas is coaxed to life through a number of other outlets including beadwork, which she has enjoyed for thirty years.

Stone, Set, Match

Anna Tollin

Who says you can't set stones amidst beadwork? This design marries the more traditional look of set stones and free-form beadwork. The result? A whimsical ring with the touch of opulence.

Materials

Faceted flat-backed stone
Prong setting
Delica beads
Assorted accent beads (seed beads, bugle beads, 4mm fire-polished beads and crystals, small pearls, stones, and sterling silver pieces)
Size B Nymo or Silamide beading thread in color to complement the Delicas

Notions

Size 12 beading needles
Scissors
Chain-nose pliers

Step 1: Set the faceted stone by placing it into the prong setting and squeezing the prongs with the pliers.

Step 2: Using 1 yd of thread, work a piece of flat peyote stitch (see "Techniques," page 105) 14 beads wide and 7 beads long. This will be the platform for the ring's top. Weave through the beads to exit from the fifth bead (make sure it's a bead that sticks "up") along the last row you stitched. Make sure your needle passes toward the center of the beadwork.

Step 3: Continue working peyote stitch off of the beadwork you created in Step 2, but this time work only 6 beads wide

and long enough so that all of the beadwork wraps comfortably around your finger. Match the beadwork to the opposite side of the piece created in Step 2—locking the beads together—and stitch the pieces together (Figure 1).

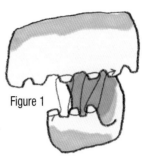

Figure 1

Step 4: Weave to the place on the platform that you'd like to set your stone. Place your setting on the beadwork and *pass through a prong. Pass down through a bead underneath the prong and weave through to the bead underneath the next prong. Continue around the setting to take it down, always hiding your thread within the beads on the platform. Exit from a bead next to the setting.

Step 5: *String 1 Delica, lay it flat on the platform, and pass through the beads that make up the platform, exiting from a bead near to where you entered. Repeat from * all around to make a close circle of beads around the setting. To further secure the setting, pass through the prongs as you go.

Step 6: Work a round of peyote stitch (see "Techniques," page 105) off of the beads you added in Step 5. If needed to reach the top of your setting, do more rounds of peyote stitch. When you are even with the top of the setting, do one more round of peyote stitch, this time making two or three decreases (see "Techniques," page 105). Pull the thread tight so that the beadwork further secures the setting. Weave through the beads to the ring platform.

Step 7: Work the rest of the ring top in a free-form fashion. Be creative as you add larger beads or different shapes into peyote or brick stitch, fringe, or other embroidery stitches. Because the ring top is so small, it's good to keep in mind that every bead is important. Small accents of color go a long way in your total design. Size 15° beads are especially useful to tuck away in small corners or add a punch of color. When finished embellishing, secure your thread and trim close to the work.

Anna Tollin, a regular contributor to Beadwork *magazine and books, lives in Minneapolis. And yes, she loves winter just so she has enough chocolate on hand. Contact Anna at annatollin@cs.com.*

Lotus Pearl Ring

Nancy Graver

This ring was devised after the designer was playing in the beads at her favorite shop. It's quick and easy to make and has been wear-tested, and it's guaranteed to make you smile!

Materials

- 3 Thai 15mm silver flowers with deep center
- 3 fresh water 12mm pearls
- Size 13 charlottes or size 14 or 15 seed beads to complement pearl color
- Fireline, 6lb test
- Burgard Studio sterling silver dangle ring

Notions

- Size 12 beading needle
- Scissors
- Thread burner

VARIATIONS

- Use smaller beads and increase the number of pearls and flowers.
- Use glass flower beads instead of silver.

Step 1: Determine which end of each pearl you'd like to face out. Make sure each pearl fits into the silver flowers.

Step 2: Using 2' of thread and leaving a 6" tail, pass through the pearl from bottom to top. String 3 charlottes and pass back through the pearl to create a picot. Pull tight and tie three square knots.

Step 3: Pass the tail and the working thread through a silver flower from inside to outside. Pass through the ring loop and all of the beads. Pass back through all of the beads and the ring loop. Tie three square knots using the working and tail threads. Repeat this step if the pearl hole width allows. Trim the thread and fuse it with the burner.

Step 4: Repeat Steps 2 and 3 to add the additional beads.

Nancy Graver, a retired CPA who lives in Lemont, Illinois, started beading in 1998 convinced that she could replicate a necklace she saw in a store for a lot less money. She hasn't turned back since.

Fleur Du Jour

Barbara L. Grainger

Wear a different flower on your finger every day! Make this amazing ring with size 11° seed beads for an impressive fashion statement or with size 15°s for a more delicate look.

Materials

Size 11° or size 15° seed beads in two colors (main color=MC, contrasting color=CC)
8mm pearl or similar accent bead
Silamide or size A Nymo thread in color to complement beads

Notions

Beading needle
Scissors
Beeswax (optional)

RING BAND

Step 1: Using 3 yd of doubled waxed thread, add a tension bead and string 6 beads, pulling them next to the tension bead. Pass back through the fifth bead just strung.

Step 2: String 3 beads and pass back through the first bead strung in Step 1 (marked in Figure 1 with a dark outline).

Step 3: String 3 beads and pass back through the second bead just strung.

Step 4: String 3 beads and pass through the center bead of the "net" in previous row (Figure 1).

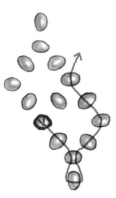

Figure 1

Step 5: Continue Steps 3 and 4 until the netting just barely fits around your finger.

Step 6: To join the strip, make sure you end on an even-numbered row. String 3 beads and pass back through the second just strung. String 1 bead (#4 on Figure 2). Making sure the strip is not twisted, bring the ends of the strip together and pass through the center bead of the first net. String 1 bead (#5 on Figure 2) and pass through the center bead of the net on the end of the strip. String 3 beads and pass through the second bead just strung. String 1 bead (#9 on Figure 2) and pass through the first bead of the strip (X on Figure 2). Remove the tension bead, secure the threads, and trim close to the work.

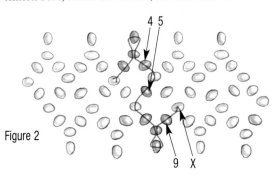

Figure 2

FLOWER TOP

Step 7: Using 1 yd of single, waxed thread, string 6 beads and tie into a circle. Working clockwise, pass through the next bead to clear the knot.

Step 8: String 10 MC and pass back through the ninth bead strung. String 3 MC and pass back through the fifth bead originally strung in this step (#5 on Figure 3). String 3 MC and pass back through the first bead strung in this step. Pass through the bead you last exited in Step 7.

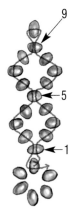

Figure 3

Step 9: Pass up through the first three beads strung in Step 8. String 3 CC and pass through the seventh–twelfth beads strung in Step 8 (#7–#12 on Figure 4). String 3 CC and pass through the fifteenth and sixteenth beads strung in Step 8, back through the first bead strung in that step, and through the next bead on the original ring from Step 7 (see Figure 4). This is your first petal.

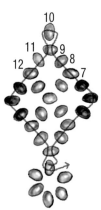

Figure 4

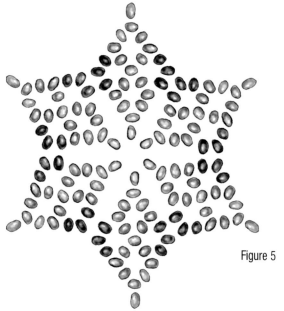

Figure 5

Step 10: Repeat Steps 8 and 9 to create five more petals (Figure 5).

Step 11: Work a second layer of petals exactly the same as the first, except offset them by working them between the beads on the original ring created in Step 7. Do so by looping around the exposed thread instead of passing through beads (Figure 6). When each petal is finished, pass through the next base bead to get into position to make the next leaf.

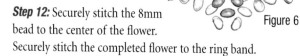

Figure 6

Step 12: Securely stitch the 8mm bead to the center of the flower. Securely stitch the completed flower to the ring band.

Barbara L. Grainger is an internationally recognized beadwork author, instructor, and designer who specializes in innovative beadwork techniques.

Sea Urchin Ring

Donna Zaidenberg

Inspired by a ring originally designed by NanC Meinhardt, this fuzzy ring begins as a flat piece of peyote-stitched beadwork and is then built up in three layers. Add a face bead and your sea urchin is all of the sudden a friend.

Materials

- Metallic-finish Delica beads
- Size 14° or 15° seed beads
- Size 1 bugle beads
- Accent beads
- Silamide beading thread or Fireline fishing line

Notions

- Size 11 or 12 beading needle
- Scissors

Step 1: Create the first layer of the ring.

Rows 1–6: Using 1 yd of thread and leaving a 6" tail, work a strip of odd-count peyote stitch (see "Techniques," page 105) 5 beads wide and 6 rows long.

Row 7: Work one-drop peyote stitch across except at the third bead position you will work two-drop, making a one-bead increase (see "Techniques," page 105).

Row 8: Work peyote stitch across.

Row 9: Work peyote stitch across, working one-drops over one-drops and a two-drop over the two-drop.

Row 10: Work peyote stitch across, making two-drop increases at the second and fourth bead positions.

Rows 11 and 12: Work peyote stitch across, working one-drops over one-drops and a two-drop over the two-drop (the edge beads, one on each side, will now be the only one-drops).

Row 13: Work peyote stitch across, making a three-drop increase at the center bead position.

Rows 14 and 15: Work peyote stitch across, working one-drops over one-drops, two-drops over two-drops, and three-drops over three-drops.

Row 16: Work peyote stitch across, making three-drop increases at the second and fourth bead positions.

Rows 17–20: Work peyote stitch across, working one-drops over one-drops, two-drops over two-drops, and three-drops over three-drops.

Row 21: Work across as the previous rows except use a different color bead as your middle bead. This is for marking purposes only.

Row 22: Work peyote stitch across as usual.

Row 23: Work peyote stitch across as usual, keeping the color change you made in Row 21.

Row 24: Work peyote stitch across as usual.

Rows 25–29: Work peyote stitch across as usual, changing the middle bead to its original color.

Row 30: Work peyote stitch across, making a two-drop decrease the second and fourth bead positions.

Rows 31 and 32: Work peyote stitch across as usual.

Row 33: Work peyote stitch across, making a two-drop decrease at the center bead position.

Rows 34 and 35: Work peyote stitch across as usual.

Row 36: Work peyote stitch across, making a one-drop decrease at the second and fourth bead positions.

Rows 37 and 38: Work peyote stitch across as usual.

Row 39: Work peyote stitch across, making a one-bead decrease at the center bead position.

Rows 40–45: Work peyote stitch across as usual.

Step 2: Work a second layer of peyote stitch over the beadwork created in Step 1. To do this, you will pass through a bead from the bottom layer and string a bead (or amount of beads required to replicate the bottom layer). Pass through the next bead on the bottom layer (this will always be the second or fourth bead position). This stitch seats the new beads not directly on top of, but in the "ditches" that lie above and below the peyote-stitched beads. This is called "beading in the ditch" (Figure 1). Working this way will give you a smaller amount of beads on the second layer—this is part of the design.

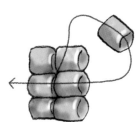

Figure 1

Note: When you reach the middle of the ring top, work in the alternate color you placed in Step 1, Row 21. When finished, exit from an outside bead at one end of the first layer.

Step 3: Work odd-count peyote stitch five beads wide off the end of the ring top to create the ring band. Make it long enough so that the ring top and band fit comfortably around your finger. Lock the beads from both ends of the beadwork together so they fit like a zipper. Stitch the ends together securely.

Step 4: Work a second layer of beads over the ring band as you did in Step 2. Secure your thread and trim close to the work.

Step 5: Embellish the ring. Do so by first trying the ring on and determining at what point on the ring top the fringe should begin. Start a thread at that point. *String 1 bugle and 1 size 15°. Pass back through the bugle and the next bead of the second layer. Repeat from * back and forth across the face of the ring so the ring top is completely covered with short fringe. Secure the thread and trim close to the work.

VARIATIONS

- Sew a small face bead to the center of the ring top before adding fringe. You will find the center of the ring top where you added the alternately colored beads in Step 1, Row 21.
- Work other non-fringe bead embroidery techniques on the ring top, using the layers of peyote stitch as your "fabric."
- Work color patterns into the second layer and don't embellish the top.

Donna Zaidenberg teaches beadwork at the national level as well as locally in the Chicagoland area through the NanC Meinhardt studio. Contact her at dlzaidenberg@aol.com.

Wonder Dome Ring

Susan Manchester

Create this elegant ring using bicone crystals to weave half of a dodecahedron—who thought geometry could be so fun? To make this sparkly math class a little easier, visualize making three interlocking flowers when you work the dome; each flower contains five petals and five seed beads in the center.

Materials

18 bicone 4mm Swarovski crystals
Size 11° metallic-finished seed beads
Spiderline or Fireline 4lb test fishing line

Notions

Size 10 beading needle
Scissors

Step 1: Using 2 yd of line and leaving an 8" tail, string 1 crystal, 1 seed bead, 1 crystal, 1 seed bead, 1 crystal, and 1 seed bead. Use a square knot to tie into a circle. Pass through the first five beads again, exiting from the third crystal added in this step.

Step 2: String 1 seed bead, 1 crystal (marked on Figure 1 as bead 4), 1 seed bead, 1 crystal (#5), and 1 seed bead. Pass through bead 3 (Figure 1). **Note:** To reinforce the weave, do another pass through the beads added in this step, bead 3, the next seed bead, and bead 4. Make this second pass when adding new beads in the following steps.

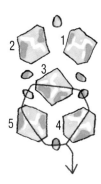

Figure 1

Step 3: String 1 seed bead, 1 crystal (#6), 1 seed bead, 1 crystal (#7), and 1 seed bead. Pass through bead 4, the next seed bead, bead 6, the next seed bead, and bead 7 (Figure 2).

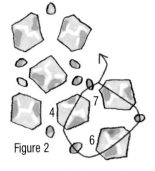

Figure 2

Step 4: String 1 seed bead, 1 crystal (#8), 1 seed bead, 1 crystal (#9), and 1 seed bead. Pass through bead 7, the next seed bead, and bead 8. You now have five petals of your first flower.

Step 5: String 1 seed bead, 1 crystal (#10), and 1 seed bead. Pass back through bead 1. String 1 seed bead and pass through bead 8, the next seed bead, and bead 10 (Figure 3). This step gives you the fifth "seed" in the center of your five-petaled flower.

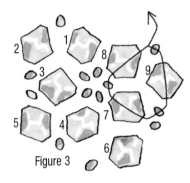

Figure 3

Step 6: String 1 seed bead, 1 crystal (#11), 1 seed bead, 1 crystal (#12), and 1 seed bead. Pass through bead 10 (Figure 4). Weave through the beads to exit at bead 12.

Step 7: String 1 seed bead, 1 crystal (#13), 1 seed bead, 1 crystal (#14), and 1 seed bead. Pass through bead 12, the next seed bead, and bead 13 (Figure 4).

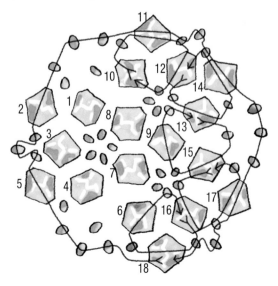

Figure 4

Step 8: String 1 seed bead, 1 crystal (#15), and 1 seed bead. Pass through bead 9. String 1 seed bead and pass through bead 13 (Figure 4). Pass through the first seed bead added in this step and bead 15 to create the fourth petal of the last flower.

Step 9: String 1 seed bead, 1 crystal (#16), 1 seed bead, 1 crystal (#17), and 1 seed bead. Pass through bead 15, the next seed bead, and bead 16 (Figure 4).

Step 10: String 1 seed bead, 1 crystal (#18), and 1 seed bead. Pass through bead 6. String 1 seed bead and pass through bead 16 (Figure 4). Pass through the first seed bead added in this step and bead 18.

Step 11: Exiting from bead 18, string 3 seed beads. Pass through the next crystal and adjacent seed bead on the perimeter of the dome. String 1 seed bead and pass through the next seed bead and crystal on the perimeter of the dome. Repeat this step twice around the dome (Figure 4). Weave through all of the beads again to reinforce. Pass through a set of three seed beads on the perimeter.

Step 12: Create a band by stringing the number of seed beads required to fit your finger. The number of beads should be a multiple of 3, plus 1 (e.g., 31, 34, 37, etc.).

Step 13: Pass through the 3 matching seed beads on the opposite side of the dome. String 3 seed beads and pass through the fourth-to-last bead strung in Step 12. String 2 seed beads, skip 2 beads on the band, and pass through the next. Continue stringing 2 beads and skipping 2 beads until there are 3 beads left on the band. String 3 seed beads and pass through the set of 3 seed beads you last passed through in Step 11. Weave through all the beads on the band twice more to reinforce. Secure your thread and trim close to work.

Susan Manchester is a corporate executive from Mound, Minnesota, who is eagerly awaiting retirement so she can spend more time beading and teaching bead classes.

Crocheted Tri-colored Stacked Rings

Leslie Venturoso

This sparkling trio of rings is made with bead crochet and glittery charlottes. They easily roll over your knuckle for maximum comfort. Whether you decide to wear one or all three together, you're certain to gather compliments!

Materials

    Size 13° in gold, silver, and copper-colored charlottes
    4mm–6mm flat focal beads (Swarovski crystal rondelle,
        button pearl, etc.)
    Jean Stitch thread in color to complement beads
    Size B or D Nymo or Silamide beading thread in color to
        complement beads

Notions

    Stringing needle (Big Eye, fine sewing needle, or twisted
        wire needle) or Bead Spinner
    #26 or #28 tapestry needle or darning needle
    Size 12 sharps or beading needle
    Size 9/1.25 mm crochet hook to match crochet thread
    Scissors

Step 1: Use the stringing needle or bead spinner to string 14" of gold charlottes on the Jean Stitch thread. Leaving a 6" tail, work in tubular bead crochet (see "Techniques," page 105) in rounds of five beads, adding one bead in each of the stitches. Crochet enough rounds so that the beaded cord fits around your finger. Lengths of 2.5" to 3" will fit most fingers.

Step 2: Join ends of the ring using the darning needle to weave tails back and forth. This is your first ring band.

Step 3: Repeat Steps 1 and 2 twice, creating two more rings—one of silver and the other of copper.

Step 4: Using beading thread and a beading needle, stitch into the copper ring at its join. Tie a knot between beads and pass through a few more. String the focal bead and a charlotte. Pass back through the focal bead and into the ring band. Continue passing back and forth through the focal bead and charlottes until the beads are secure. Tie a knot between beads, pass through a few more, and trim close to the work.

Step 5: Use beading thread and a needle to embellish the other two rings at their joins. You can add focal beads or do free-form bead embroidery with charlottes as shown in the photo.

Leslie Venturoso visited her local bead shop just four years ago to get help fixing a favorite necklace. One bead led to another and she hasn't stopped beading since. Leslie lives in Davie, Florida, does commissioned works, and teaches classes. Contact her at Lesliebeads@aol.com.

Furry Knuckles

Dustin Wedekind

Adding fringe to beadwork is a fun way to create texture, and patterned fringe is even more exciting! These rings begin with a square-stitched base that is then embellished with a matching pattern. Animal prints are an obvious choice for this furry fringe, but you can use any pattern and give it this extra level of motion.

Materials
   Delica beads
   Size 14° seed beads
   Size D beading thread
   Thread Heaven

Notions
   Size 11 beading needle
   Scissors

Step 1: Using 4' of conditioned thread, string a tension bead leaving a 4" tail. String Delicas for the first row of the pattern, which is the ring's band width (Figure 1).

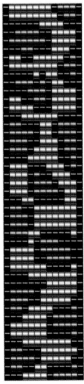

Figure 1

Step 2: Use square stitch (see "Techniques," page 105) and follow the pattern to make a band long enough to wrap around your finger.

Step 3: To begin the fringe, pass through the first bead on the previous row. * String 5 size 14°s the same color as the Delica you just passed through. Slide the beads down to the band and hold them and the thread in place with your left thumb. Skipping the last bead, pass back through 4 beads and the next Delica (Figure 2). Be sure that the fringe leg is snug to the band. Repeat from * across the whole row, but don't place a fringe on the last Delica.

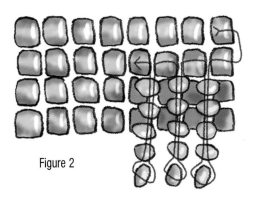

Figure 2

Step 4: Repeat Step 3 to fill the top of your ring—about ¾". After the final row of fringe, weave back to the first row of the base. Use square stitch to join the ends of the bracelet to form the ring.

Dustin Wedekind is the senior editor for Beadwork *magazine.*

Layered Elements

Linda Leibsker

This elegant ring is a snap to make! The components work up quickly in square and brick stitches and you just need to sew them together to finish it off. Change the colors and sizes of the beads for completely different looks.

Materials

Sizes 8°, 11°, and 15° seed beads
2mm focal bead (freshwater pearl, triangle bead, etc.)
Silamide beading thread

Notions

Size 10 and 11 sharps beading needles
Scissors

Step 1: Using 1 yd of thread, the size 11 needle, size 11° beads, and leaving a 4" tail, work a base row of ladder stitch (see "Techniques," page 105) 7 beads wide. Pass through all seven beads again to reinforce the row.

Step 2: Work brick stitch (see "Techniques," page 105) to create six rows off the base row you created in Step 1. Decrease 1 bead each row so you end up with a triangle. Weave through the beads to exit from the first bead of the foundation row.

Step 3: Repeat Step 2 on the other side of the foundation row to form a diamond shape. Secure your thread and trim close to the work.

Step 4: Repeat Steps 1–3, this time beginning with a five-bead ladder-stitched foundation row. Weave through the beads to the center of the diamond but do not cut the thread.

Step 5: String the focal bead and a size 15°. Pass back through the focal bead and into the foundation row of the small diamond. Place the large diamond under the small one and pass through the large diamond's foundation row. Pass up through the small

diamond again and back down through the large diamond until the two diamonds are securely fastened. Set the diamonds aside.

Step 6: Using 2 yd of thread, the size 10 needle, size 8° beads and, leaving a 4" tail, work a square-stitched (see "Techniques," page 105) ring band 4 beads wide and long enough to fit comfortably around your finger. Reinforce the band by passing through all the beads again and recheck the fit. Exit from an outside bead at the end of the band.

Step 7: Use size 11° beads to embellish the two long sides of the ring band with a picot edging. Begin by stringing 3 beads. Pass between the next two size 8°s of the ring band so you loop the exposed thread. Pass up through the third bead just strung. String 2 beads, pass between the exposed thread

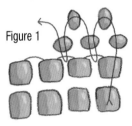

Figure 1

between the next two beads on the ring band and up through the second bead just strung (Figure 1). Repeat this step across the ring band's edge. Weave to the opposite edge of the band and embellish with this picot edging.

Step 8: Weave to a center bead at the middle of the band. Sew the diamond top created in Step 5 to the band by passing through the center bead of the element's foundation rows. Weave to the next bead on the foundation row and pass back through the center of the band to secure. Weave through beads to exit near the outside of the diamond. Pass up through the beads on the perimeter of the larger diamond and down through the band to secure the entire perimeter of the diamond. Reinforce all of the stitches to hold the diamonds securely to the band. Weave to an outside bead at the end of the band.

Step 9: Fold the band so the beginning and end meet. Square-stitch the first and last rows together to create a circle. Fill in the picot edge on each side. Reinforce the ring by passing through all the beads again if needed. Secure the thread and trim close to the work.

Linda Leibsker is a bead artist who also teaches and designs jewelry crafts for seniors. She lives in Chicago, Illinois.

Buttercup

Betcey Ventrella

This lovely flower ring seems a little tricky to make at first, but once you've got the hang of it you can easily make one for each finger.

Materials

- 5 round 4mm Swarovski crystals
- 5 lentil 6mm Swarovski crystals
- 5 bicone 4mm Swarovski crystals
- Size 11° seed beads in color to complement crystals
- 2 crimp tubes
- Fireline
- 4" of .05mm Stretch Magic jewelry elastic

Notions

- Size 12 beading needle
- Scissors

Step 1: Using 4' of thread, string 1 round, 1 lentil, 1 bicone, and 1 lentil. These are beads 1–4 on Figure 1. Pass through all again, exiting from bead 4. Tie a square knot and trim the tail end close to the work. Pass through beads 1 and 2 again to clear the knot.

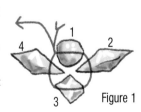

Figure 1

Step 2: String 1 bicone (#5), 1 lentil (#6), and 1 round (#7). Pass through beads 2, 5, and 6 (Figure 2).

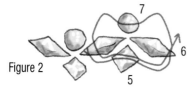

Figure 2

Step 3: String 1 round (#8), 1 lentil (#9), and 1 bicone (#10). Pass through beads 6, 8, and 9 (Figure 3). String 1 bicone (#11), 1 lentil (#12), and 1 round (#13). Pass through beads 9, 11, and 12 (Figure 3).

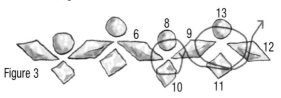

Figure 3

Step 4: String 1 round (#14) and pass through bead 4, connecting the beads into a circle (Figure 4).

Figure 4

Step 5: String 1 bicone (#15) and pass through beads 12 and the last bicone (Figure 5). Reinforce and tighten the circle by passing through the all the bicone crystals once. Pass through one of the lentils, and reinforce and tighten the round crystals by passing through all of them.

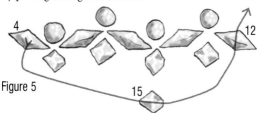

Figure 5

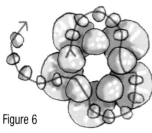

Figure 6

Step 6: String 5 seed beads, skip the next round crystal, and pass through the next one. Continue around the circle making "petals" (Figure 6). Once you've added seed beads around all 5 crystals, reinforce them by passing through all again. Exit from the second seed bead added in this step.

Figure 7

Step 7: String 3 seed beads and pass through the fourth seed bead added in Step 6. Pass through the next 3 seed beads so you exit from the second seed bead of the next petal (Figure 7). Repeat around to add 5 picots in all. Reinforce all by passing through all of the seed beads.

Step 8: If your flower is still floppy at this point, reinforce it by passing up through one of the lentils, through the adjacent bicone, and back down through the next lentil. Pass through the round crystal, back up the next lentil, through the adjacent bicone, and so on. Weave to the seed bead petals and to the second bead added in Step 6.

Step 9: String 6 seed beads and pass through bead 4 (see Figure 7). Reinforce by passing through all just strung. Weave to the opposite side of the flower. Because this is a five-petal flower, there isn't an exact opposite, so you'll have to improvise a bit in deciding which seed beads to exit from. Add 6 seed beads on this side as you did on the other. Weave through a few more beads, secure your thread, and trim close to the work.

Step 10: Use the elastic to string a crimp tube. Pass the end through one of the loops created in Step 9, then back through the crimp tube leaving a ½" tail. Squeeze the tube neatly and tightly using crimping pliers and trim the short tail close to the crimp tube.

Step 11: String about 20–30 seed bead onto the elastic. Because it is difficult to string the size 11's on the elastic, use a beading tweezers to pick the seed beads one at a time to place them on the end of the elastic. Test the fit around your finger and adjust accordingly. String a crimp tube, pass through the other loop created in Step 9, and back through the crimp tube. Pull all snug, crimp neatly, and trim close to the work.

Betcey Ventrella is the all-knowing goddess of Beyond Beadery in Rollinsville, Colorado. Contact her at (303) 258-9389; betcey@beyondbeadery.com; www.beyondbeadery.com.

Beaded Cluster Ring

Lisa Gettings

Here's a cocktail ring for the twenty-first century! Large and funky, it's perfect to make on a Saturday afternoon just before heading out to dance the night away.

Materials

16–20 faceted 4mm Czech fire-polished beads or Swarovski crystals
1' of 14-gauge sterling silver wire or purchased ring band
1 spool of 24-gauge, non-tarnish silver Artistic Wire

Notions

Flush cutters
Chain-nose pliers
Ring mandrel
G-S Hypo cement glue

Step 1: Wrap the 14-gauge sterling silver wire around the ring mandrel at a half size larger than your ring size. Overlap the wire on the top by about one-third of the circumference of the ring and cut (Figure 1).

Figure 1   Figure 2

Step 2: Secure the overlapped section using 1 yd of 24-gauge wire. Do so by leaving one end of the wire several inches longer than the other and wrapping it tightly around the overlapped portion of the ring base (Figure 2).

The longer length of wire will be used to add the beads on top of the wrapped and over-

lapped section. Place a few drops of glue on the wrapped section of the ring and allow it to dry.

If you are using a purchased ring band, cut a yd of 24-gauge wire, leaving one end of the wire several inches longer than the other, and wrap tightly around the "top" of the ring band.

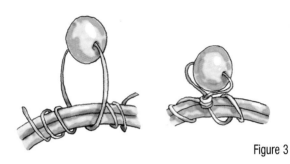

Figure 3

Step 3: String a bead on the long piece of wire. Anchor it about ¼" above the wrapped base by bending the wire down on each side of the bead. Twist the bead and wire two to three times while holding down the long length of wire in place. This will firmly anchor the bead on top of the base (Figure3).

Step 4: Wrap the wire one time around the base to further secure the bead and string another bead. Repeat the twist-and-wrap process across the entire wrapped base, making sure to place the beads in a clustered pattern.

Step 5: When you are pleased with the shape and beads added to the base, anchor the ends of the remaining wire in between the beads. Find a tight spot and weave the wire carefully around several beads. Trim the wire close to the ring, making the ends as inconspicuous as possible.

Step 6: Cut 2' of 24-gauge wire. Anchor one end of the wire at one end of the beaded cluster. Wrap the wire tightly and uniformly along the rest of the bare base to the other side of the beaded cluster. Neatly anchor the wire and trim close to the work.

Lisa Gettings lives in Seattle and teaches at Fusion Beads. Lisa credits her mother Linda, a frequent project contributor to Beadwork, *for her addiction to beading. More about this mother-daughter bead-venture can be found at www.beadgeneration.com.*

Galaxy Ring

Cindy Reiland

You'll be reminded of the cosmos every time you wear this light and whimsical ring. Use colorful wire and beads to make this design, and you'll be well on your way to designing your own galaxies … if only in miniature!

Materials

- 6mm focal bead (crystal or Czech fire-polished bead)
- Assorted 2mm–4mm beads (crystals, pearls, Czech fire-polished beads, etc.)
- 20-, 22- or 24-gauge colored Artistic Wire, depending on the width of bead holes

Notions

- Wire cutters
- Round-nose pliers with jaw protectors
- Flat-nose pliers with jaw protectors
- Ring mandrel (or large dowel the width of your finger)

Note: If your wireworking tools don't have jaw protectors, dip them in Tool Magic tool coating and let them dry 2–3 hours before using.

Step 1: Cut a piece of wire 14"–16" long. Beginning at the center of the wire, make three tight coils around the mandrel at your ring size. Finish by making both wire ends point in the same direction (Figure 1). **Note:** As you wrap, take care to lay the coils next to one another, not overlapping them. This is your ring band.

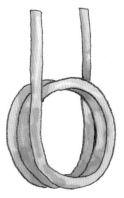

Figure 1

Step 2: Slide the coils off the mandrel and carefully hold the ring back with the flat-nose pliers. Use your fingers to wrap each wire end tightly onto the coils, ending with both wire ends pointing in the same direction (Figure 2).

Figure 2

Step 3: String your focal bead on one of the wire ends and place it across the top of the ring band. Secure it by passing the wire under and over the ring band.

Step 4: Weave both ends of the wire randomly around the top and sides of the ring, adding beads and curves of wire. Anchor the wire every ½"–1" of the wire, always passing under and over a previous curve. Take care when creating the curves to make smooth transitions so that the wire won't catch on anything when it is worn. When you near the end of the wire, curve it under a lower or hidden wire and secure it by forming a loop. Finish the other wire end in the same fashion.

Cindy Reiland has been beading eight years, mostly to escape her other life as a math teacher. She lives in Minnesota with her husband and three cats, Lobelia, Jaybird, and Chulie.

Glitterati

Jean Campbell

This ring is flashy, fashionable and, best of all, adjustable. It's so easy to make you won't want to tell your admirers it didn't come from Bulgari.

Materials

- 4mm faceted Czech fire-polished beads
- 6mm rhinestone
- Ring-sized memory wire

Notions

- Needle-nose pliers
- Memory wire cutters

Step 1: Use the pliers to bend back one end of the memory wire. Pinch the bend shut so that the wire lays back on itself (Figure 1). This bend will act as a stopper for your beads.

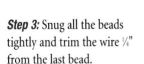

Figure 1

Step 2: String twenty 4mms, the rhinestone, and twenty 4mms.

Step 3: Snug all the beads tightly and trim the wire ¼" from the last bead.

Step 4: Repeat Step 1, bending this end of the wire.

Jean Campbell is the editor-in-chief of Beadwork *magazine.*

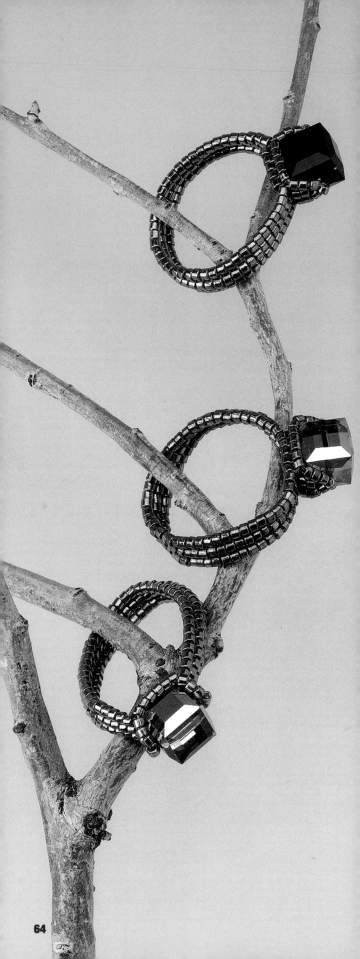

Hip to Be Square

Diane Fitzgerald

A Swarovski crystal cube is the focal point for this fashionable ring. It is made with a band of square stitch, three rows wide, and with two short rows added to support the base of the crystal.

Materials

    1 Swarovski crystal 8mm cube bead
    3 g Delica beads in color to complement crystal
    Size D Nymo thread

Notions

    Size 12 sharps needles
    Scissors

Step 1: Using 2 yd of thread, string 4 Delicas. Pass through all beads again, exiting the fourth bead strung. Do not knot. Hold the beads upright in a square (Figure 1) to begin square stitch (see "Techniques," page 105).

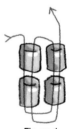

Figure 1

Step 2: String 2 Delicas. Pass down through two beads on the left, and work up through three beads on the right (Figure 2).

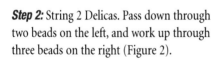

Step 3: Working with a loose tension, repeat Step 2 until the length of the band fits around your finger at the widest part of the knuckle. Work a third row of square stitch along the length of the band.

Step 4: Weave through the outer row of beads until you have reached the halfway point. Form a base for the crystal cube by

Figure 2

working five beads of square stitch on each side of the ring band at this mid-point (Figure 3).

Figure 3

Step 5: Exit from the end bead in the outer edge row of five beads. String 3 Delicas, the crystal cube, and 3 Delicas. Weave back and forth through these beads 4 times.

Step 6: Exit the cube bead, add 2 Delicas, and pass through the five beads of the center row of the cube base. String 2 Delicas, and pass through all of these beads again.

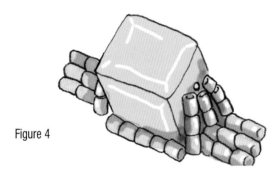

Figure 4

Step 7: Exit the cube bead, add 3 Delicas, and pass through the five beads on the remaining 5-bead edge 4 times (Figure 4). Add 1 Delica to cover the cube hole on both sides, if desired.

Step 8: Weave through the band to an outer edge. Join the rows to form the ring band by weaving back and forth. Secure the thread and trim close to work.

Like many of us, Diane Fitzgerald is addicted to beads. You may reach her at dmfbeads@bitstream.net.

Darla Ring

S. Raven Willey

Inspired by a piece worn by the character "Darla" on the television series Buffy the Vampire Slayer, this ring can be adapted to your own mood by changing the colorway or center bead.

Materials

    1 red glass heart or round 6mm bead
    2 round 4mm red crystals or glass beads
    Size 15° copper seed beads
    Size 11° black seed beads
    Power Pro 10lb test

Notions

    Fiskar's child-size scissors
    Size 12 sharps needles

Step 1: Using 1 yd of thread with a needle at each end, use the first needle to string 1 size 15°, the center glass heart or round bead, 1 size 15°, and 6 size 11°s (beads 1–6 in Figure 1). Center these beads on the thread. Pass the first needle through the first size 15° strung, the heart, and the second size 15° strung.

Step 2: Using the second needle, string 6 size 11°s (beads 7–12 in Figure 1), pass through the size 15° at the bottom of the heart, the heart, and the remaining size 15°. There should be a needle exiting each of the size 15°s.

Step 3: Using the first needle, string 3 size 15°s. Pass back through the size 15° at the base of the heart and through the heart bead. Do not pass through the top size 15°. Repeat this step with the second needle. (See Figure 1.)

Step 4: Using the first needle, pass through the size 11°s of the circle to exit from the fourth bead. String 2 size 11°s (beads 13 and 14 on Figure 1) and square-stitch (see "Techniques," page 105) them to the third and fourth size 11°s of the seed bead circle.

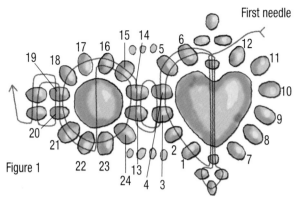

First needle

Figure 1

15 14
17 16
19 18
6
12
11
10
9
8
7
20
21
22 23
13
24 4 3
5
2
1

Step 5: With the first needle exiting from the second bead of the square-stitched pair, string 10 size 11°s (beads 15–24 in Figure 1). Pass through beads 13–17 to form a circle of 12 seed beads.

Step 6: Use the first needle to string one 4mm bead. Pass back through beads 23–19.

Step 7: String 2 size 11°s. Square-stitch them to beads 20 and 19 (Figure 1).

Step 8: Continue by creating a strip of two-wide square stitch that will make up half of the ring band length.

Step 9: Repeat Steps 3–8 using the second needle to weave the other side of the ring.

Step 10: When the two square-stitched bands are the correct length for your finger, square-stitch the ends together. Weave each needle back through the band to bead 16 on each side of the ring.

Step 11: Use one of the needles to string 3 size 15°s. Pass through bead 6, the heart, and bead 1. String 4 size 15°s and pass through bead 23. Weave your thread through several beads to strengthen the beadwork. Secure the thread and trim this thread close to the work.

Step 12: Repeat Step 11 for the other side of the ring.

S. Raven Willey is Howling Rabbit and has hosted several bead retreats and workships in southwestern Pennsylvania and has plans for more in the future. You can contact Raven through her website, www.howlingrabbit.com

You Won't Do Dishes in This Ring

Leslie Granbeck

This sparkling beauty starts with a simple, tubular peyote band. Add beads and lots of fringe for a textured, finger-top garden you'll want to wear everywhere but in the kitchen.

Materials

Size 11° Japanese seed beads
10mm or smaller focal bead (oblong pearl, lampworked bead, pressed glass bead, etc.)
Size 15°–size 6° seed beads in a variety of colors
Small accent beads (freshwater pearls, drops, flowers, leaves, cubes, 3mm or 4mm crystals)
Size B Nymo or Silamide beading thread

Notions

Size 12 beading needles
Thread conditioner
Scissors

Step 1: Using 4' of well-conditioned thread, string an even number of size 11°s to fit your finger. For a size 7 ring, string 44–48 beads. Adding or subtracting 2 beads will change the ring size by about a half ring size. Tie the beads into a circle, leaving an 6" tail. Slip the band on your finger to check the size. Keep in mind that the finished ring will be a little smaller than the original circle when completed. Adjust the number of beads as needed.

Step 2: Work up to 7 rounds of single-drop tubular peyote stitch (see "Techniques," page 105), depending on how wide a ring band you'd like. Weave in tail thread to secure and trim close to the work.

Step 3: Create an enlarged base for the front of the ring. Start by peyote-stitching enough beads to cover about one-third of the circumference of the entire band. Turn your direction so that you now are working flat peyote stitch. Decrease the length of the next four to six rows to create a tapered- or diamond-shaped base (Figure 1). Weave through the beads to the other side

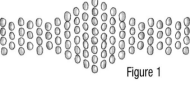

Figure 1

of the band and repeat this step. **Note:** This beading platform does not have to be the same shape on both sides of the ring (one side could be triangular, the other side square). If preferred, the platform can be added only to one side of the ring.

Secure your thread and trim close to the work.

Step 4: Begin a new thread within the ring's front. Place the focal bead off-center, passing through it several times to secure. If the height of the bead means that the thread will show, string seed beads on either side of it before you stitch it down.

Step 5: String enough seed beads to reach across the focal bead. Stretch it across the bead and into the beadwork of the platform. If you wish, weave up to two rows of single-drop peyote stitch along this strand to further enhance and stabilize the focal bead in place.

Step 6: Add additional small beads to the platform around the focal bead, knotting the thread after two to three beads for added security.

Step 7: Surround the focal bead with clumps of fringe. Plan this fringe as for a garden: Place short fringe around a taller neighboring clump. Loops and chunky spikes will add texture. For short fringe, exit a bead in the platform base and string up to 4 seed beads. Pass through all but the last bead strung. Weave through an adjacent bead in the platform to secure.

Step 8: Continue adding beads and fringe until the entire platform is covered.

Step 9: Reinforce the ring band by weaving through it several times. Also reinforce any fringe legs that are heavy or contain sharp beads, such as crystals. Secure the thread and trim close to the work.

Leslie Granbeck has been beading and teaching bead-weaving techniques for nearly ten years. She enjoys being part of the vibrant, creative, sometimes crazy, community of beaders in Minneapolis, Minnesota, and beyond.

Sister Lucien

Betcey Ventrella

When you wear this ornate ring you'll receive more compliments than you'll know what to do with! But it's not just pretty, it's smartly constructed. The top is made with thread that just won't break, and the elastic cord band makes it very comfortable.

Materials

- 1 oval 9x6mm crystal
- 12 round 3mm crystals
- 2 g of size 15° seed beads
- 20 size 11° seed beads to complement ring top
- 2 crimp tubes
- Fireline
- 4" of .05mm Stretch Magic jewelry elastic

Notions

- Crimping pliers
- Size 12 sharps or beading needles
- Beading tweezers
- Scissors

Step 1: Using 4' of thread, string a tension bead (see "Techniques," page 105), leaving a 4" tail. String 1 size 15°, the oval crystal, and 11 size 15°s.

Step 2: Pass through the crystal, skipping the first size 15° (Figure 1). String 11 size 15°s and pass through the first seed bead strung in Step 1 so that there is a ring of seed beads around the crystal.

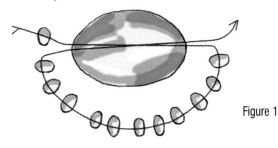

Figure 1

Step 3: Reinforce the entire circle of seed beads by passing through each size 15° twice. Trim the tail and tension bead.

Step 4: Pass through one of the seed beads, string 3 size 15°s, skip 1 seed bead on the base round, and pass through the next seed bead (Figure 2).

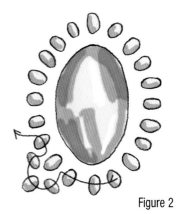

Figure 2

Step 5: Repeat Step 4 around the circle until you have 12 small triangles (Figure 3).

Step 6: Pass through one of the outer points of a triangle, string one 3mm crystal, and pass through the next triangle tip. Continue around until you have added 12 crystals.

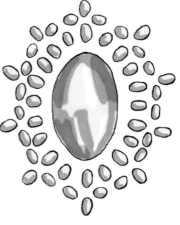

Figure 3

Step 7: *String 1 size 15°. Pass through the next 3mm crystal. Repeat from * around the circle (Figure 4).

Step 8: Pass through one of the seed beads added in Step 7. String 4 size 15°s and pass through the next seed bead added in Step 7. Continue around the circle, adding 4 seed beads at a time (Figure 5). Reinforce by passing through all of the seed beads in this outer round.

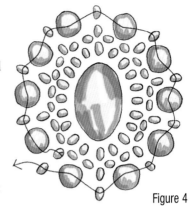

Figure 4

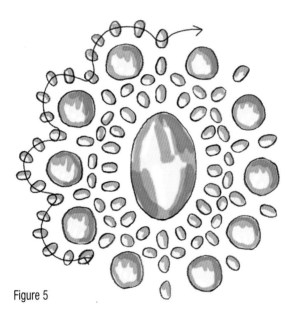

Figure 5

Step 9: Create two loop sides for the ring band. There are two crystals on each side of the larger crystal. Exit from one side, string 6 size 15°s, pass back through the top of the next round, then pass through several times to reinforce. Weave the Fireline through several seed beads and secure with two half hitch knots. Pass the needle through the beads to the other side of the ring top. Create a second loop side, reinforce, and secure. Trim remaining Fireline close to the ring top.

Step 10: Cut a 4" piece of Stretch Magic. String a crimp tube. Thread the elastic through the middle of one of the seed bead loops created in Step 9 and pass back through the crimp tube. Gently crimp the tube and trim the tail close to the tube.

Step 11: String enough size 11°s so that the beads and the ring top fit around your finger. It may be difficult to string the seed beads onto the elastic, so try using beading tweezers. When the band is large enough, string another crimp tube and pass the elastic through the loop on the other side, and back through the crimp tube. Snug the beads and gently crimp the tube. Trim the elastic close to the work.

Betcey Ventrella is the all-knowing goddess of Beyond Beadery in Rollinsville, Colorado. Contact her at (303) 258-9389; betcey@beyondbeadery.com; www.beyondbeadery.com.

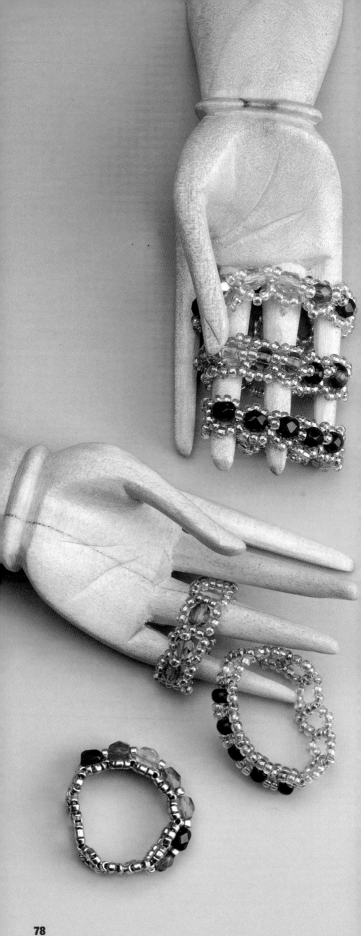

Chakra Ring

Sue Swanson

Need a little healing? Make and wear these right-angle woven rings on your fingers or toes to help you focus on your chakras—the seven energy fields of the body. When your chakras are aligned, you'll be healthier in mind, body, and spirit … people will see it in your smile!

Materials

Size 11° seed beads or Delica beads
7 Czech 4mm fire-polished beads, one each in red,
    orange, yellow, green, blue, indigo, and violet
Nymo D beading thread to complement the seed beads
Thread Heaven

Notions

2 size 12 beading needles
Scissors
Clear nail polish

Step 1: Using 4' of well-conditioned thread, string 12 size 11°s, leaving an 8" tail. Use square knots to tie in a circle. Pass through the first 9 beads just strung.

Step 2: String 9 size 11°s. Pass through the seventh through ninth beads strung in Step 1 and the first six beads just strung (Figure 1). This is single-needle right-angle weave.

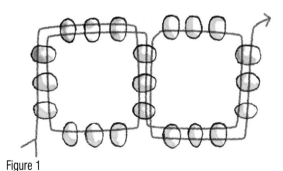

Figure 1

Step 3: String 9 size 11°s. Pass through the fourth through sixth beads strung in the previous step and the first six beads just strung.

Step 4: Repeat Step 3 until the ring fits snugly on your finger. A ring with 10 to 12 loops will fit most women. Note that the loops give slightly to accommodate the knuckle.

Step 5: Close the circle of right-angle weave by stringing 3 size 11°s and passing back through the first three beads added in Step 1. String 3 size 11°s and pass through the fourth through sixth beads strung in the last loop (Figure 2).

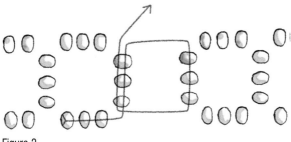

Figure 2

Step 6: Reinforce the band by weaving through all of the loops in the same pattern you initially stitched them. End by passing up through the fifth bead added on one of the loops.

Step 7: String the red 4mm. Pass up through the fifth bead added in this same loop to seat the 4mm snugly within the beadwork. Repeat this step, adding 4mms to consecutive loops in the proper chakra order: red, orange, yellow, green, blue, indigo, and violet (Figure 3). When you have added your last 4mm, weave through all of the seed beads in the next loop on the band and pass back through the violet bead.

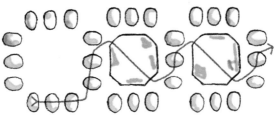

Figure 3

Step 8: String 1 size 11°. Pass back through the next 4mm. Repeat across to add a size 11° between each 4mm.

Step 9: Weave through several loops on the band. Secure your thread and trim close to the work. Apply clear nail polish to any knots and let dry.

Sue Swanson is a bead artist and teacher from Woodbury, Minnesota. She is a member of the Upper Midwest Bead Society. Contact Sue at swansonMN4@aol.com.

The 7 Chakra Points

Root/Base	Red
Sex/Navel	Orange
Solar Plexus	Yellow
Heart	Green
Throat	Blue
Brow	Indigo
Crown	Violet

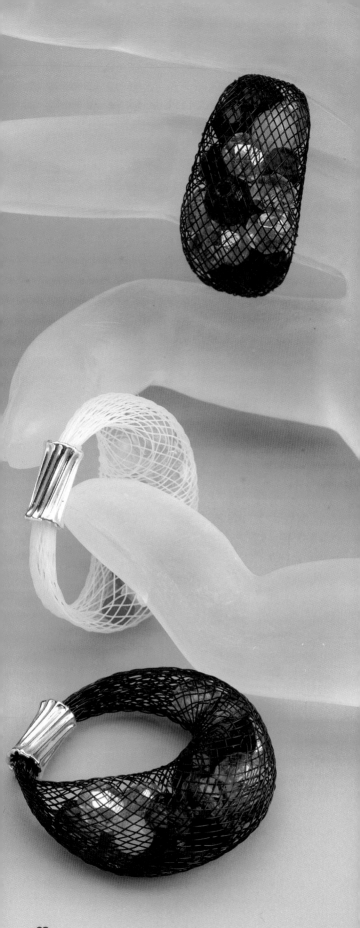

In-Mesh Ring

Mary Libby Neiman

Want to make a statement? It's simple to do when wearing this ring. It's easy to make and once you're done you can still make adjustments—just firmly squeeze the mesh to remove a bead; gently press a bead into the mesh to add one.

Materials

In-Mesh tubular netted fabric
Short oblong bead with a 4mm hole
12–15 assorted 4mm–6mm glass beads
Thread to match mesh color
Elmer's All-Purpose glue
Tape

Notions

Size 8 or 9 sharps needle
Tape
Scissors
Small binder or alligator clamp

Step 1: Cut 4½" of mesh. Wrap tape tightly around one end of the mesh, compressing the mesh as small as possible.

Step 2: String the oblong bead over the taped end. Place the 12 to 15 assorted glass beads into the mesh tube.

Step 3: Wrap the mesh tube around your finger so it fits. Make a note as to where the mesh should be trimmed when finished for a good fit.

Step 4: Use the clamp to close the open end of the mesh. Sew the end closed, stitching through the compressed mesh near the clamp. Make several stitches and wrap the thread firmly around the stitched area. Sew several more stitches, knotting the thread onto itself to finish. Trim the thread and remove the clamp.

Step 5: Untape the first end of the mesh, and manipulate it to open it fully. Keeping in mind how much of initial 4½" of mesh must be trimmed, insert the stitched end into the untaped end. If the overlap is longer than the oblong bead, trim the first end until the overlap will fit into the oblong bead.

Step 6: Stitch the overlapped areas together and end by wrapping the thread very tightly around the stitched area, knotting the thread onto itself to finish. Apply the glue to the stitched area. While the glue is still moist, slide the oblong bead over to cover the glued area. Wipe off any excess glue.

Chicagoan Mary Libby Neiman has always been intrigued with manipulating fibers, whether weaving, braiding, knitting, crocheting, or spinning/plying. Adding beads to fibers has expanded this interest to the point of obsession. Contact her at marylibby@onsurface.com.

Spring Ring

Laura Funk

Nothing beats wearing a ring to put a little spring in your step. Using tightly spaced fringe, create a ring that places a pretty pastel garden at your fingertips, or substitute metallic stars for a holiday party look.

Materials

Size 6° assorted green seed beads
Size 11° clear green seed beads, to complement size 6°
    beads
Size 11° opaque white seed beads
10–15 small accent beads: flowers, stars, drop beads
Power Pro, .006 10lb test

Notions

Size 11 English beading needles
Thread Heaven conditioner
Scissors

Step 1: Using 4' of well-conditioned Power Pro, string two size 6° seed beads and tie them together, leaving a 6" tail. The beads should be flat and touching each other, with the holes facing up. Pass up through one of the beads, leaving the tail on the bottom.

Step 2: String a size 6°. Pass up through the last bead you exited and down through the bead just strung. This is ladder stitch (Figure 1). Continue adding size 6°s until the strip fits across the top of your finger. For a size 7–8 ring this will be five beads long.

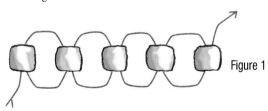

Figure 1

Step 3: Continue to do ladder stitch until you've doubled the length you created in Step 2. Fold the strip in half so that the holes of the beads are all face-up. Stitch each set of the side-by-side beads together so that you end up with a two-bead wide strip (Figure 2).

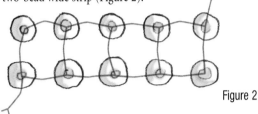

Figure 2

Step 4: Exit down through an end bead in the base strip and string enough size 6° beads to make the rest of the ring band. Pass up through the other end of the base strip at the bead opposite the bead you just exited. Pass down through the adjacent base strip bead and string enough size 6° beads to make the rest of the ring band. Pass up through the remaining end bead at the other end of the base strip. Reinforce the base strip and band by weaving through all several times. Exit from an end bead on the face of the base strip.

Step 5: Embellish the ring base. String three size 11°s and pass back through the second and first beads just strung and back into the ring base bead to create a leg of fringe. Pass up through the next size 6° to make another leg of fringe (Figure 3). Continue across the base strip, adding fringe legs to make the ring face look full. You can vary the fringe by adding accent beads or more seed beads. Put longer fringe toward the middle of the base strip so that it is supported by the shorter fringe around the outer edge.

Figure 3

To finish, tie a knot between beads, weave through a few, tie another knot, and trim close to the work.

Laura Funk has been accused of being a high maintenance "girly girl." In reality, she lives in Woodbury, Minnesota, and enjoys a variety of crafts, especially her newfound love of beading.

Sculptural Flower Ring

Diane Fitzgerald

This springy flower ring isn't just bloomin' pretty—it's also a wonderful conversation starter! Just alter the colors of the petal and center beads to vary the look.

Materials

    Delica beads in two colors (A and B)
    8mm round pearl or faceted bead
    Nymo D beading thread in color to complement beads
    Future Acrylic Floor Polish

Notions

    Size 12 beading needle
    Scissors
    Thin cardboard
    Paper toweling

Step 1: Using 1½ yd of double and waxed thread, create a strip of ladder stitch (see "Techniques," page 105) using color B that is 3 beads wide and long enough to wrap around your finger. Join the ends. Do so by passing through the first row and then again through the last row twice. Secure the thread and trim close to the work. Set aside.

Step 2: Using 1 yd of single waxed thread, create a strip of ladder stitch 2 beads wide and 16 beads long using color A. This will be your flower base.

Step 3: With your thread exiting the last bead on the base,

string 2 A. Pass down through the second column of beads in the ladder and up through the first column of beads, exiting from the first bead just strung (Figure 1).

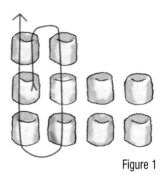

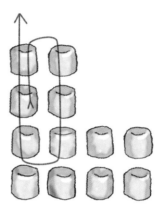

Figure 1

Step 4: String 2 A. Pass down through the next 2 Delicas on the second column and up through 3 on the first column (Figure 2). Repeat this step until you have added 5 rows above the base. This is your first petal.

Step 5: To finish the petal, string 3 A. Pass down through two beads in the second column and up through two beads in the first column. Pass through the beads just strung and down through the entire second column. Pass up through the next column (Figure 3).

Figure 2

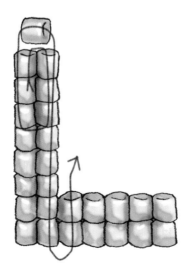

Figure 3

Step 6: Repeat Steps 4 and 5, creating the remaining 7 petals.

Step 7: Join the ends of the base row to form a circle and stitch them together by passing through the first two beads of the base row and the last two beads twice.

Step 8: String the 8mm, seat it in the middle of the petals, and *pass through the beads at the opposite side of the base. Pass up through two beads in the next column of the base and back through the 8mm. Repeat from * to secure the 8mm.

Step 9: Securely stitch the flower to the outside of the band created in Step 1.

Step 10: Stiffen the flower and band by dipping them in the floor polish. Roll the cardboard into a long thin tube and place the band on it. Set the ring flower-side-down on your paper towel-covered work surface so that the petals flare out. Let dry for 24 hours.

Like many of us, Diane Fitzgerald is addicted to beads. You may reach her at dmfbeads@bitstream.net.

Cube Bead Ring

Lynn Krestel

This simple, square-stitched design is easy to make out of stretch cord, yet goes from funky to sophisticated just by changing the beads. Be sure to choose beads that have a large enough hole for the stretch cord to pass through more than once.

Materials

42–50 Miyuki 3mm cube beads
9 Czech fire-polished 4mm beads
1½ yds of clear 0.5 m stretch beading cord

Notions

Thin flexible beading needle, if desired
G-S Hypo Cement or clear nail polish

Step 1: Use the cord to string 6 cubes, leaving half of the length of the cord as the tail. String 1 fire-polished, 1 cube, 1 fire-polished, 1 cube, and 1 fire-polished. Finish this first row by adding enough cubes to reach the desired ring length. This row, called Row 1, will become the middle row of the ring.

Step 2: String 2 cubes. Pass through the second-to-last and last bead of those strung in Step 1 and through the two just strung. This will create a square of beads. Pull the cord snug to begin shaping the rows of the ring band. String 1 cube and pass through the adjacent bead from those strung in Step 1. Pass through the bead just strung. This is square stitch (Figure 1). Continue working square stitch, adding cubes next to cubes and fire-polished next to fire-polished. The cord should exit from the last bead strung. This row, called Row 2, is your first outside row.

Figure 1

Step 3: Using the original tail from the first row, work square stitch on the other side of the original row as you did in Step 2. This row, called Row 3, is your second outside row.

Step 4: Using the tail from Row 2, pass through the first and second beads of the Row 2 and back through the two adjacent end beads of Row 1 to turn the band into a circle. Using the tail from Row 3, pass through the first and second beads of the Row 3 and back through the two adjacent end beads of Row 1 (Figure 2). The tails should now meet. Tie the tails in a square knot, and pull snugly. Turn the ring 180 degrees, and tie another square knot. Add a drop of cement and trim tails close to the work.

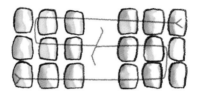

Figure 2

Lynn Krestel has been beading for more than four years, and loves creating jewelry. Her website, budsandbeads.com, is under construction.

Flower Power Ring

Jamie Hogsett

You can make these wire rings in a flash! Not only quick, they're an excellent project to learn French beaded wire techniques. Try stacking a few on one finger for a fun "corsage" look.

Materials

Size 11° Czech seed beads
Magatama beads
26-gauge Artistic Wire

Notions

Nylon-jaw pliers
Wire cutters
Ring mandrel
Chain-nose pliers

Step 1: Unwind 16" of wire from the spool, but do not cut it. Use the nylon-jaw pliers to straighten out any kinks in the wire. You can do this any time during the making of the ring to keep the wire strong and workable.

Step 2: String 8" of seed beads onto the spool of wire.

Step 3: String 3 magatamas. Hold these three beads and slide the seed beads down the spool of wire, leaving at least 4" of wire free of beads. Slide the magatamas so that they are 2" from the end of the wire. Grasp the wire on both sides of the magatamas and twist the wire so the beads end up in a tight circle. This is the center of the flower. Keep the 2" end of wire below the flower at all times.

Step 4: Bring 16–20 seed beads toward the magatamas. (The more seed beads you use, the bigger the petals will be.) Leaving a tiny amount of wire between the magatama twist and the seed beads, bring the spool end of the wire to this small area and twist the wires to form the first petal. Repeat four times to make five petals.

Step 5: Slide enough seed beads up to the flower to fit around the correct size on the ring mandrel. Leaving a small amount of wire between the flower and the seed beads of the band, bring the spool end of the wire to this small section and twist.

Step 6: Move the petals so they are evenly spaced and positioned correctly around the center of the flower.

Step 7: Cut the spool end of the wire even with the 2" length of wire left in Step 1. Holding the two wire ends together, twist a few times around the base of the flower at the top of the ring band to keep everything in place. Cut the wire close to the base and tuck the ends in using the chain-nose pliers.

Jamie Hogsett is projects editor for Beadwork *magazine.*

Pretty Pearl Ring

Sara Beth Cullinan

When you make this ring, you'll capture the mystery of the ocean floor with its undulating coral formations and its occasional prize—a pearl. Don't let the design fool you; it's really quite simple if you carefully study the illustrations below.

Materials

Size 11° seed beads
22 bicone 3mm Swarovski crystals or Czech fire-polished beads
1 baroque 8mm glass pearl
Size D Nymo beading thread in color to complement beads

Notions

Size 12 beading needles
Scissors

Step 1: Create the beginning of the ring top.
Round 1: Using a comfortable length of thread, string 3 seed beads and tie into a circle with a square knot leaving a 12" tail (Figure 1).

Figure 1

Round 2: *String 2 seed beads and pass through the next bead from Round 1.
Repeat from * around, exiting from the first two beads added in this round (Figure 2).

Round 3: *String 1 seed bead and pass through the next seed bead from the previous round.
Repeat from * around, exiting from the first bead added in this round (Figure 3).

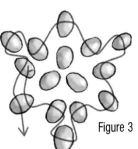

Figure 2

Round 4: *String 2 seed beads and pass through the next

Figure 3

bead from the previous round. Repeat from * around, exiting from the first two beads added in this round (Figure 4).

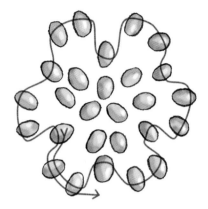

Figure 4

Rounds 5–8: *String 1 seed bead and pass through the next bead from the previous round. Repeat from * around, exiting from the first bead added in each round (Figure 5). Keep a firm tension throughout. By Round 7 your beadwork will curl up to form a basket.

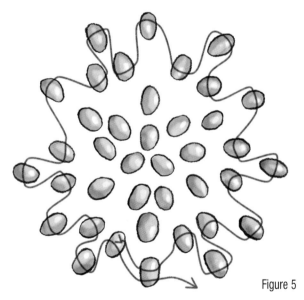

Figure 5

Step 2: Add a needle to the thread's tail and pass up through the bottom of the beadwork. String the pearl and 3 seed beads. Pass back through the pearl and into a seed bead on the beadwork. Seat the pearl into the basket. Pass through the pearl and seed beads a few times to reinforce the connection. Secure the thread and trim close to the work.

Step 3: Using the working thread, weave through the bead-work to exit from one of the beads added in Round 5. String 1 seed bead and pass through the next bead added in Round 5. String 1 seed bead and pass through the next bead added in Round 5. String 1 seed bead and pass through the second bead added in this step. Continue working peyote stitch (see "Techniques," page 105) off of the basket to create the ring's band. When the band and ring top slide snugly over the knuckle of your finger, attach the band end to the opposite side of the basket and weave through beads to reinforce. Secure the thread and trim close to the work.

Step 4: Begin a new thread where you left off at Step 1, Round 8.
Round 9: *String 1 seed bead, pass through the next bead from the previous round, string 2 seed beads, pass through the next bead from the previous round. Repeat from * around, exiting from the first bead added in this round.
Round 10: *String 2 seed beads and pass through the bead or set of two beads added in the previous round. Repeat from * around, exiting from the first two beads added in this round.
Round 11: *String 1 seed bead and pass through the next bead added in the previous round. Repeat from * around, exiting from the first bead added in this round.
Round 12: *String 2 seed beads and pass through the next bead added in the previous round. Repeat from * around, exiting from the first two beads added in this round.
Round 13: String one 3mm and pass through the next 2 beads added in the previous round. Repeat from * around, exiting from the first bead added in this round.
Round 14: String 2 seed beads and pass through the next 3mm added in the previous round. Weave through the last round again. Secure the thread and trim close to the work.

Sara Beth Cullinan is a frequent contributor to Beadwork *magazine and has also been featured in other bead related publications. She divides her time between beading and belly dancing in sunny Arizona. She can be reached at sarabeth44@msn.com.*

Why Wear Diamonds?

Lea Zinke

Why wear diamonds when you can adorn your hand with beautiful lampworked beads like these? Constructing this ring is so easy that you'll want to move all your lampworked beads out of your bead box and onto your fingers!

Materials

1 lampworked bead, 6mm–10mm with a design on the top side, flat on the reverse side
2 bead caps to fit lampworked bead
2 bicone 2mm–3mm crystals to complement the lampworked bead
10–15 sterling silver 2mm–3mm triangular beads
Size 0.8mm clear stretch cord

Notions

Scissors
G-S Hypo Tube Cement

Step 1: Using 12" of cord and leaving a 4" tail, string the lampworked bead, 1 bead cap, 1 crystal, and 12 sterling silver beads. Wrap the strand around your finger and add or subtract silver beads so that the band fits, allowing for a second crystal and bead cap. String 1 crystal and 1 bead cap.

Step 2: Tie a surgeon's knot and cinch tight. Place a drop of glue on the knot. Pass one of the ends of the cord through the lampworked bead. Gently pull on that end of the cord until the knot is hidden in the hole of the lampworked bead.

Step 3: With the first loose end of the surgeon's knot cord, tie a cinch knot onto the band of the ring, and dot with glue. Repeat on other side of the ring with the other loose end.

Step 4: Allow the knots to dry fully. Finish by passing the ends of the cord through the bead caps and also through the accent beads, if possible. Trim the loose ends close to the beads.

Lea Zinke is a glass artist who has been creating garden-inspired, lampworked art glass beads for more than five years. Lea lives in Clearwater, Florida, and can be reached through her website, www.leazinke.com.

VARIATION

Instead of a lampworked bead at center of ring, substitute a flat-backed bead or a double-drilled flat-backed bead for a double-strand band.

Techniques

STARTING A NEW THREAD

There's no doubt that you'll run out of thread as you work on your necklaces that use off-loom stitches. It's easy to begin a new thread. There are a couple of solutions. I prefer the first way because it's stronger.

Solution 1: Tie off your old thread when it's about 4" long by making a simple knot between beads. Pass through a few beads and pull tight to hide the knot. Weave through a few more beads and trim the thread close to the work. Start the new thread by tying a knot between beads and weaving through a few beads. Pull tight to hide the knot. Weave through several beads until you reach the place to begin again.

Solution 2: Here's how to end your old thread without tying a knot. Weave the thread in and out, around and around, through several beads and then trim it close to the work. Begin a new thread the same way, weaving the end of the thread in and out, around and around, and through several beads until you reach the place to begin again.

PASS THROUGH VS. PASS BACK THROUGH

Pass through means to move your needle in the same direction as the beads have been strung. Pass back through means to move your needle in the opposite direction.

TENSION BEAD

A tension bead holds your work in place. To make one, string a bead larger than those you are working with, then pass through the bead twice, making sure not to split your thread. The bead will be able to slide along, but will still provide tension to work against.

Peyote stitch

This stitch can also be referred to as gourd stitch.

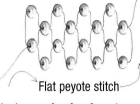
Flat peyote stitch

One-drop peyote begins by stringing an even number of beads to create the first two rows. Begin the third row by stringing one bead and passing through the second-to-last bead of the previous rows. String another bead and pass through the fourth-to-last bead of the previous rows. Continue adding one bead at a time, passing over every other bead of the previous rows.

Two-drop peyote is worked the same as above, but with two beads at a time instead of one.

Peyote stitch increase

Make a *mid-project increase* by working a two-drop over a one-drop in one row. In the next row work a one-drop peyote between the two-drop. For a smooth increase, use very narrow beads for both the two-drop and the one-drop between.

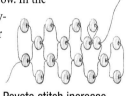
Peyote stitch increase

Peyote stitch decreases

To make a *row-end decrease*, simply stop your row short and begin a new row. To make a hidden row-end decrease, pass through the last bead on a row. Weave your thread between two beads of the previous row, looping it around the thread that connects the beads. Pass back through the last bead of the row just worked and continue across in regular flat peyote. To make a *mid-project decrease*, simply pass thread through two beads without adding a bead in the "gap." In the next row, work a regular one-drop peyote over the decrease. Keep tension taut to avoid holes.

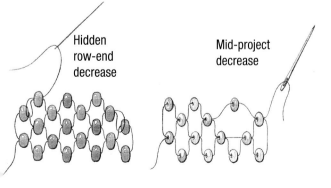
Hidden row-end decrease

Mid-project decrease

Tubular peyote stitch

Begin by determining the diameter of the form you wish to cover. Thread an even number of beads to fit in a circle over this form. Make a circle by passing through all the strung beads twice more, exiting from the first bead strung. String one bead and pass through the third bead of the first round. String one bead and pass through the fifth bead of the first round. Continue adding one bead at a time, skipping over one bead of the first round, until you have added half the number of beads of the first round. Exit from the first bead of the second round. Slide the work onto the form. String one bead, pass through the second bead added in the second round and pull thread tight. String one bead and pass through the third bead added in the second round. Continue around, filling in the "spaces," one bead at a time. Exit from the first bead added in each round.

Odd count peyote stitch

Begin by stringing an odd number of beads (our example shows five). These beads will become the first and second rows. Begin the next row by adding a bead and passing through the second-to-last bead just strung, bead 4 in our example. Continue as with even-count peyote. When you reach the end of the row, pass through beads 1, 2, and 3. Pass through the second-to-last bead in what has now become the third row. Pass back through beads 2 and 1 (in that order). Pass through the last bead added in row 3. Continue across row 4 in regular peyote. Start row 5 as you began row 3. At the end of row 5, exit from the last bead added and loop thread through the outer edge threads (not beads) of the previous row. Pass back through the last bead added and continue across the row adding one bead at a time.

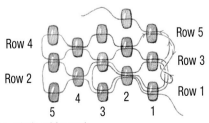

Peyote stitch odd count

Brick stitch

Begin by creating a foundation row in ladder stitch (see below). String one bead and pass through the closest exposed loop of the foundation row. Pass back through the same bead and continue, adding one bead at a time.

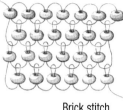

Brick stitch

Brick stitch decrease

To make a row-end decrease, string two beads to start off the row. Skip the first exposed loop and pass through the second loop. Continue across the row in regular brick stitch. Begin the next row in regular brick stitch. When adding the last bead, pass through the first bead of the previous row (rather than the exposed loop). Pass through the first and second beads of the row before that. Pass back through the first bead of the previous row, then pass back through the last bead just added.

Brick stitch decrease

Ladder stitch

Using two needles, one threaded on each end of the thread, pass one needle through one or more beads from left to right and pass the other needle through the same beads from right to left. Continue adding beads by criss-crossing both needles through one bead at a time. Use this stitch to make strings of beads or as the foundation for brick stitch.

Ladder stitch

Square stitch

Begin by stringing a row of beads. For the second row, string 2 beads, pass through the second-to-last bead of the first row, and back through the second bead of those just

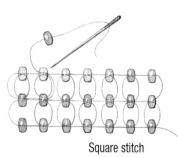

Square stitch

strung. Continue by stringing 1 bead, passing through the third-to-last bead of the first row, and back through the bead just strung. Repeat this looping technique across to the end of the row. *To make a decrease,* weave thread through the previous row and exit from the bead adjacent to the place you want to decrease. Continue working in square stitch.

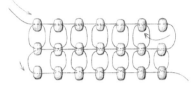

Square stitch decrease

Wireworked loop

Grasp one end of the wire with round-nose pliers. Holding on to the wire with one hand, gently turn the pliers until the wire end and wire body touch. Create a 90-degree reverse bend where they meet.

Wireworked loop

Netting

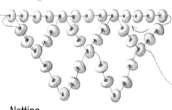

Netting

Begin by stringing a base row of 13 beads. String 5 beads and go back through the fifth bead from the end of the base row. String another 5 beads, skip 3 beads of the base row, and go back through the next. Rep to end of row. PT the fifth, fourth, and third beads of those just strung, exiting from the third. Turn the work over and go back across the same way.

Simple fringe

Exit from your base. String as many beads as you wish the finished length of the fringe leg to be. Skipping the last bead strung, pass back through all of the beads. Pass through the base and exit from the next spot on the base. Repeat across to make many legs of fringe.

Simple fringe

Bead crochet

Beaded crochet cord makes a great finish or a strap for other beadwork. Make an initial chain of four (or more) stitches, leaving a bead in each chain stitch by sliding a bead close to the hook before making each stitch. Form a ring of beaded stitches by inserting the hook into the first chain stitch, under the thread carrying the bead. Move the bead to the right of the hook.

Bead crochet

Slide a new bead down close to the hook and work a slip stitch by pulling a loop of thread through both the loops on the hook. Make a slip stitch with a bead into each of the remaining chain stitches to complete the first round. Continue working beaded slip stitches in a spiral to the length desired.

Bead knitting

Bead knitting, knitting one bead into one stitch, is the technique to use for knitting charted designs. Insert the needle into the stitch to be knit as usual, slide the bead up against the needle, and pull the bead through to the front as you complete the stitch.

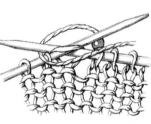

Bead knitting